MINECRAFT

ENGLISH
OFFICIAL WORKBOOK
AGES 8-9

**JON GOULDING
AND DAN WHITEHEAD**

INTRODUCTION

HOW TO USE THIS BOOK

Welcome to an exciting educational experience! Your child will go on a series of adventures through the amazing world of Minecraft, improving their written English skills along the way. Matched to the National Curriculum for writing for ages 8–9 (Year 4), this workbook takes your child into fascinating landscapes where our heroes Kim and Sami embark on building projects and daring treasure hunts…all while keeping those pesky mobs at bay!

As each adventure unfolds, your child will complete topic-based questions worth a certain number of emeralds . These can then be 'traded in' on the final page. The more challenging questions are marked with this icon to stretch your child's learning. Answers are included at the back of the book.

MEET OUR HEROES

Kim is one of the best warriors in the world – or at least that is what she likes to tell people! She always wants to craft the best weapons and armour and will explore far and wide to find rare materials. Although Kim is not yet the legendary fighter she claims to be, she is loyal and brave and will defend her friends from mobs, no matter how deadly!

Sami just loves to wander. He is incredibly curious and is always the first to dig into an interesting looking cave, or dash into a new biome to see what he can find. He sometimes forgets to think a situation through before carrying out his actions, but he can always rely on help from his friend Kim!

First published in 2021 by Collins
An imprint of HarperCollins*Publishers*
1 London Bridge Street, London, SE1 9GF

HarperCollins*Publishers*
1st Floor, Watermarque Building, Ringsend Road, Dublin 4, Ireland

Publisher: Fiona McGlade
Authors: Jon Goulding and Dan Whitehead
Project management: Richard Toms
Design: Ian Wrigley and Sarah Duxbury
Typesetting: Nicola Lancashire at Rose and Thorn Creative Services

Minecraft skins courtesy of Claudia 'ZestyKale' Faye

Special thanks to Alex Wiltshire, Sherin Kwan and Marie-Louise Bengtsson at Mojang and the team at Farshore

Production: Karen Nulty

ISBN 978-0-00-846283-3
British Library Cataloguing in Publication Data.
A CIP record of this book is available from the British Library.
1 2 3 4 5 6 7 8 9 10
Printed in the United Kingdom

MOJANG STUDIOS

MIX
Paper from
responsible source
FSC
www.fsc.org
FSC™ C007454

This book is produced from independently certified FSC™ paper to ensure responsible forest management.

For more information visit: www.harpercollins.co.uk/green

CONTENTS

FOREST RESOURCES

Explorers will never run out of materials in a forest biome. Conditions are good for trees to grow and thrive so wood is always in supply. Lots of different flower types grow here as well.

ENEMIES AMONG THE TREES?

There is the constant threat of enemy mobs lurking even in the daytime, with the shade of the trees protecting them from sunlight. However, explorers can find and tame a wolf to give themselves better protection.

EYES ON THE OCEAN

The sun shines through the trees, making the flowers look even brighter and more colourful than usual as Kim wanders through the forest. Where had she not explored yet? The ocean! She would need a lot of preparation for this expedition.

PREFIXES

The prefix *in-* usually means *not* (for example: *indefinite* means not *definite*). The prefix *in-* changes depending on the spelling of the word it is added to. For example, if the word begins with *l*, then *in-* becomes *il-*. Before a word beginning with *m* or *p*, *in-* changes to *im-*. Before a word starting with *r*, *in-* becomes *ir-*.

Kim begins to make a list of the things she will need to explore under the sea. Maybe she should try to find Sami? He could help.

 1

Match each prefix to the correct word.

il-	im-	in-	ir-

perfect	definite	regular	legal

2

Choose the best word from the box to complete each sentence.

impossible	irresponsible	incorrect	illegible

a) It would be .... to enter the forest without preparation.

b) The trees were tall and some looked .... to chop down.

c) Kim found an old wooden sign but the writing was ....

d) If Kim thought she was completely safe, she was ....

SUFFIXES -SURE AND -TURE

Words which end with the same sound that appears at the end of *treasure* often have the spelling *-sure*. Words which end with the same sound as *picture* often have the ending *-ture*.

Kim tries holding her breath. She can only manage it for a short time. To swim to the bottom of the ocean, she will need a Potion of Water Breathing. Where can she get one?

1

Draw lines to join the start of each word on the top row to the correct ending on the bottom row.

furni	trea	mea	adven

ture	sure

2

Choose the best word from the box to add to each sentence.

nature	creature	treasure	adventure

a)   Kim thought she saw a strange .... in the trees.

b)   Exploring the ocean would be an exciting ....

c)   It was great to be walking in ....

d)   She remembered that potions can be found in buried ....

Kim will need to buy an explorer map from a villager to lead her to a treasure chest. If she is lucky, there will be a Potion of Water Breathing inside.

3

Complete the word in each sentence, using *-sure* or *-ture*.

a) Kim would like to build an enclo................ where she can keep animals.

b) It is a plea................ to walk through the forest.

c) Kim would like to build a struc................ to store her materials.

d) She tries to pic................ what it will be like under the ocean.

4

Find out what each of the words below means. Write a definition for each word, and a short sentence containing that word.

a) capture ....

....

b) leisure ....

....

WORD ENDINGS SOUNDING LIKE ZHUN

You should already know that a verb is a word to describe an action or a state and that a noun is a word for a place, person or thing. Many verbs ending in -se or -de have the ending -sion when changed into a noun form. For example, *divide* (a verb) changes to *division* (a noun). The *-de* (or -se) ending is removed and *-sion* is added. These words have a *zhun* sound at the end, as is heard at the end of *division*.

Kim piles up some dirt blocks and climbs high up to see over the trees. She is in luck! There is a village not too far away.

1

Change each of the verbs below to a noun with the *-sion* ending that gives a *zhun* sound.

a)   confuse ....   b)   televise ....

c)   revise ....   d)   exclude ....

2

Choose the best word from the box to use in each sentence.

occasion	decision	vision	confusion

a)   Kim needed to make a .... about which direction to take.

b)   There was .... about the best way to reach the village.

c)   On this .... she knew exactly what to do.

d)   She had a .... of what she might find in the ocean.

As she makes her way to the village, Kim sees a creeper blocking her path. Then she spots some zombies as well. This journey just got a lot harder. Take care, Kim!

3

Remove the *-sion* ending from each noun below and replace it with *-de* or *-se* to form the verb.

a) inclusion ....

b) conclusion ....

c) provision ....

d) erosion ....

4

 Remove the *-sion* ending from each of the nouns in the box and replace it with the *-de* or *-se* ending to create the verb form. Then add the appropriate verb to each sentence.

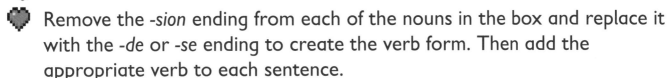

| evasion | explosion | intrusion | revision |

a) There were so many mobs, Kim thought

her mind would ....

b) These enemies were going to

.... on Kim's adventure.

c) She might need to .... her plans.

d) Kim would need to .... the

zombies while she defeated the creeper.

WORD ENDINGS SOUNDING LIKE *SHUN*

Although the *-sion* word ending often sounds like *zhun* as in *division*, it can also make a *shun* sound as in *extension*. Other word endings such as *-tion*, *-cian* and *-ssion* make the same sound. The ending *-tion* is most common if the root word ends in *-t* or *-te*. The ending *-ssion* is common if the root word ends in *-ss* or *-mit*. The ending *-sion* usually replaces *-d* or *-se* endings on root words, and *-cian* usually replaces *-c* or *-cs* root word endings.

Eager to get on with her quest for an explorer map, Kim throws herself into battle against the creeper and the zombies. Go get them, Kim!

1

Draw lines to join each word to the correct *shun* sounding ending.

| music | express | inject | expand |

| -sion | -tion | -ssion | -cian |

2

Choose the best word from the box to use in each sentence.

| fiction | action | hesitation | mathematician |

a) Kim could multiply and divide well, and could be described as a good

....

b) She knew her sword would see .... when she spotted the zombies.

c) She attacked without ....

Kim defeats the enemies and makes her way to the village. One of the villagers is a cartographer, which means she can finally buy a map.

3

Remove the *shun* sounding ending from each word and correctly write the root word beside it.

a) permission ....

b) action ....

c) magician ....

d) comprehension ....

4

Look at the nouns *attention* and *intention* below. Their root words both end in *-d* but, rather than a *-sion* ending, they have *-tion*. Write a Minecraft-themed sentence using either the noun or one of the other forms of it shown in brackets.

a) attention (attend / attended / attending) ....

....

b) intention (intend / intended / intending) ....

....

 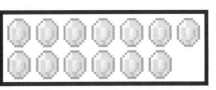

COMMON MISSPELLINGS

Many words can have unusual spellings or spellings that are easy to confuse with other spelling patterns. It is important to be able to recognise the spelling of these words.

The cartographer villager will only trade an explorer map for emeralds and a compass. Kim has enough emeralds, but no compass. She will need to find some redstone dust and iron ingots to craft one.

1

In each of the words in the box, the s sound is spelled using c. Underline the s sound and write each word in the correct sentence.

centre	decide	noticed

a) Kim .... a promising spot for mining close to the village.

b) She had to .... where to start digging for redstone.

c) She dug a hole in the .... of the forest.

2

Each of the words below has the same unpronounced (silent) letter. Underline this letter in each word.

a) guide   b) build   c) tongue   d) guilty

Kim digs deep into the ground and discovers a cave with redstone and iron ore in the walls. Unfortunately, it also has spiders and lava!

3

The spelling *augh* can make different sounds. Read each word in the box. Use each word to replace an underlined word with which it rhymes in the sentences below.

caught	**laugh**	**taught**

a) A spider fell into the lava, which made Kim <u>giraffe</u>.

....

b) She would make sure those spiders were <u>sort</u> a lesson.

....

c) Kim needed to make sure she was not <u>sport</u> in the cobwebs.

....

4

Think about the words *busy* and *business*.

a) What is unusual about the spelling of one sound common to both words?

....

b) Write a sentence about mining redstone using one or both of the words.

....

....

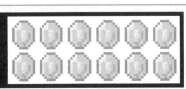

DICTIONARIES AND HOMOPHONES

A dictionary can be used to check the spelling and the definition (the meaning) of words. Knowing the first few letters of a word helps when looking for it in a dictionary because words are sorted by the alphabetical order of their first letter and, if the first letter is the same, by their second letter and so on.

Kim hurries back to the surface and quickly crafts a compass from the materials she has mined. She returns to the village and buys the explorer map. Now to find some buried treasure!

 I

Write these words in alphabetical order.

| spider | shelter | Sami | structure |

 2

Use a dictionary to find and write the definitions of these two words.

a) foe ....

....

b) foliage ....

....

The explorer map directs Kim to a beach. It is a long way away. Kim checks that she has food and weapons and starts walking.

3

Homophones and near-homophones are words that sound the same or very similar but have a different spelling and meaning. Rewrite each pair of homophones in alphabetical order.

a)   seen / scene   ....

b)   mail / male   ....

c)   meet / meat   ....

d)   grown / groan   ....

4

Use a dictionary to help you write sentences that include the near-homophones below.

a)   accept ....

....

except ....

....

b)   affect ....

....

effect ....

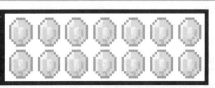

THE **I** SOUND SPELT **Y**

In some words, the short *i* sound as in *pit* is represented by a *y*.

Kim walks and walks through the forest. It seems to go on forever! Suddenly she hears a noise close by.

 I

Circle the short *i* sound in each of these words.

a) symbol   b) Egypt   c) gym

d) cygnet   e) rhythm   f) hymn

2

Choose the best word from the box to use in each sentence.

myth	mysterious	sorry	oxygen

a) Kim heard something .... in the trees.

b) She needed the Potion of Water Breathing to give her

.... in the ocean.

c) Sami once told her a story about a gigantic forest monster but that was

just a ....

It is getting dark, which means that dangerous mobs will be on the prowl. Through the shadows Kim spots a skeleton. Has it seen her?

3

Write the correct spelling of each underlined word in the passage below.

As she gazed at the <u>Lyly</u> of the Valley flowers, Kim knew trouble was coming.

> [blank box]

Like a <u>gimnast</u>, she climbed a tree to get a better view. It was just <u>tipical</u> that

> [blank box]   [blank box]

there was a skeleton nearby when she needed to rest. If only she had a <u>cristal</u> ball

> [blank box]

to see what would happen next in this adventure.

4

Using each word below, create sentences about this Minecraft adventure. Use a dictionary if you are unsure of the meaning of the words.

a) mystery ....

....

b) symbol ....

....

c) myth ....

....

WORDS FROM OTHER LANGUAGES

Many of the words used in everyday English have their origins in other languages (such as French, Greek and Latin).

Kim does not have time to waste! She runs to attack the skeleton before it can shoot her with its arrows.

1

The *ch* in two of the words below sounds like the *k* in *kick*. Find these words and write them in the spaces provided.

The noise from Kim's battle echoed around the forest, although there were only a few chickens to hear it. She was a strong fighter and would surely defeat the skeleton. Sitting on a birch tree stump afterwards, Kim came up with a scheme for success.

....

2

Many words that use the *ch* spelling to make the *sh* sound heard in *shop* come from French. Find the two words using *ch* in this way in the text below. Write down the words and include a definition for each of them.

Kim felt like a great chef when she used the chicken to give her more health. She wished she had a time machine so she could check what her next adventure would be.

....

....

Kim can now see the edge of the forest and the sandy beach just beyond. This has been an epic trek but she has made it!

3

The *gue* with a *g* sound and the *que* with a *k* sound that are found at the end of words also come from French. Choose the word from the box that best fits into each sentence.

unique	**technique**	**fatigue**	**league**

a) This was such a special, ... adventure.

b) Kim's success in battle was down to her excellent sword skills and

    ....

c) She was in a .... of her own when it came to exploring.

d) Kim needed a rest because .... was setting in.

4

Write a definition for each of the words below.

a) antique ....

b) vague ....

Kim arrives at the beach just as the sun is rising. She will rest for a while and then start looking for the treasure.

 5

The *sc* spelling of the *s* sound heard in *sit* has its origins in Latin. Find and write the three words using the *sc* spelling of the *s* sound in the passage below.

Kim could smell the scent of the sea and, after a decent rest, she felt very relaxed taking in the beautiful scenery. It was fascinating for her to see the glittering blue ocean that stretched out in front of her.

....

....

6

Look at the two words below. Write them into a sentence (or two) about Kim climbing up and down a tree. Use a dictionary to help you.

| ascend | descend |

....

....

....

....

....

....

COLOUR IN HOW MANY EMERALDS YOU EARNED

ADVENTURE ROUND-UP

WONDERS OF THE WATER

Kim looks out at the ocean in front of her, and cannot help wondering what incredible creatures and amazing treasures she might find at the bottom.

TREASURE TO FIND

To get to the bottom of the ocean, Kim will need to be able to hold her breath for a lot longer, so she gets up and begins to search for the buried treasure chest, hoping a Potion of Water Breathing will be inside.

VOCABULARY, GRAMMAR AND PUNCTUATION

SUN, SEA AND SAND

Wherever the land meets the sea, you will usually find a beach. You can try to get a suntan if you like, but it is more fun to explore.

BEACH BOUNTY

There may be a shipwreck poking out of the water, or you may find a friendly turtle to hang out with. One thing is for sure, whether it is a small sandy strip or a huge sun-kissed paradise, beaches are the best place to find buried treasure!

TREASURE HUNT

Kim's explorer map has led her to the beach. If she can find a Potion of Water Breathing in a buried treasure chest then she will be ready to explore beneath the waves.

ADDING CLAUSES

A clause is part of a sentence and it contains a subject (what the sentence is about) and a verb (an action). For example: *Kim saw a zombie.* Sentences are often made more interesting by using more than one clause. Clauses are joined with conjunctions (*and, but, or, if, when, because,* etc.). For example: *Kim saw a zombie <u>when</u> stepping out of the shelter.*

The map shows Kim exactly where to dig, but that's for later.

 1

Join each clause on the left to the most suitable additional clause on the right.

Kim decides to explore the beach and	it would be useful to have a companion.
Her inventory was heavy because	Kim would still need a good sense of direction.
The explorer map was useful but	she starts to walk across the hot sand.
Kim could explore alone although	it was full of useful items.

2

Complete each sentence below, adding a conjunction and a second clause.

a) The beach was sandy ....

....

b) Kim thought it looked beautiful ....

....

STANDARD ENGLISH

Standard English is the English that is recognised around the world, using correct grammar and with a formal or polite tone for speaking or writing. Non-standard English is the English often used in everyday conversations with people we know. Grammar rules are often ignored and slang (informal words) is often used.

As she explores the beach, Kim spots a turtle. She is very excited. Turtles are one of her favourite animals!

1

Kim introduces herself to the turtle. Tick the option written in Standard English.

"Hiya turtle." ☐

"Hi there turtle. What ya doing?" ☐

"Good morning turtle. I am Kim." ☐

"Hey turtle. I'm Kim, who are you?" ☐

2

Read each sentence and place a tick in the correct column: S (if it is in Standard English) or NS (if it is in Non-standard English).

Sentence	S	NS
Kim were walking along beach.		
Kim was walking along the beach.		
Kim was walking on beach.		

Kim decides to call the turtle Turpin. She enjoys watching Turpin go about its business. What a happy life it seems to have.

3

Rewrite each sentence using Standard English or more formal writing.

a) Turpin fancied a dip in the sea.

b) What's it looking at?

c) The beach is proper ace.

d) There is loads and loads of sand.

4

Kim writes a note to Sami to tell him about her arrival at the beach. Read part of the letter below and rewrite it using Standard English.

The journey were well good. Bet I have to scrap with summat though soon. I reckon I'll find loads of dead cool treasure.

COLOUR IN HOW MANY
EMERALDS YOU EARNED

DETERMINERS

Determiners give more detail about a noun. Some determiners are not specific (for example: _a_ zombie) but others state which noun (for example: _that_ zombie). Determiners can also specify quantity (for example: _some_ zombies) or possession (for example: _my_ zombie or _Kim's_ sword). Remember that the determiners _a_ and _an_ depend on the spelling of the word they come before.

Kim spots some seagrass growing in the shallow water. She can use that to make Turpin follow her. She wades in and picks some.

1

Choose the correct determiner, _a_ or _an_, for each word below.

a) .... beach

b) .... sandy beach

c) .... excellent beach

d) .... incredible beach

2

Circle the incorrect determiner in each sentence. Write the correct determiner below each incorrect one.

Under an blue sky, Kim walked into the shallow water. She spotted an seagrass.

It was growing in a sand in the water. Kim wondered if there was an shipwreck

or a underwater ruin in a ocean she was admiring.

As Kim paddles back to shore with the seagrass, she hears a noise behind her. Oh no! A drowned is right behind her!

3

Choose a suitable determiner from the box to use in each sentence.

some	a	Kim's	the

a) Kim saw .... drowned behind her.

b) Nearby there were .... rocks where she could hide.

c) .... drowned was approaching fast.

d) .... sword was ready in her hand.

4

For each determiner given below, write a sentence about Kim's adventure which uses that word correctly.

a) those ....

....

b) that ....

....

c) this ....

....

d) every ....

....

NOUNS AND PRONOUNS

Personal pronouns such as *he, she, it* and *they* are used in place of nouns to avoid repetition in writing. For example: *The beach was deserted and <u>it</u> was peaceful.* Possessive pronouns such as *mine, theirs, yours, hers* and *his* can also be used when something belongs to someone already mentioned in a sentence. For example: *Kim needed to find a new sword because <u>hers</u> was broken.*

Kim knows the drowned will attack Turpin if it gets too close. She has to defend her new buddy.

1

Underline the personal pronoun in each sentence.

a)   The drowned was angry and it was getting closer.

b)   Kim watched the drowned and she was ready to fight.

c)   The sea was deep and Kim thought something else moved in it.

d)   Kim and the drowned faced each other and they began to battle!

2

Replace the underlined nouns with the correct personal or possessive pronoun.

Kim had to win this fight because <u>Kim</u> did not want Turpin the turtle to be hurt.

The beach was beautiful but she wished <u>the beach</u> was safer. She had no shelter of her

own but someone had been here before and she could see <u>their shelter</u>. Kim

wondered who <u>the person</u> might be.

Kim defeats the drowned but she is worried there will be more.
Holding the seagrass, she lures Turpin over to the abandoned shelter.

3

Choose the correct possessive pronoun from the box to use in each sentence.

yours	ours	theirs	hers

a) Kim thought the shelter was abandoned. It was now _____.

b) The turtles lived on the beach and Kim realised it was _____ .

c) Kim remembered when Sami gave his sword to her and said,

"Take it. It is now _____."

d) Kim once found a cake with Sami and she said, "This cake is now

_____."

4

 Write a sentence using each of the pronouns below.

a) mine _____

_____

b) she _____

_____

c) them _____

_____

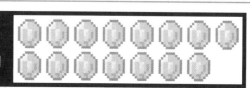
COLOUR IN HOW MANY
EMERALDS YOU EARNED

NOUN PHRASES AND PREPOSITIONAL PHRASES

Writing is made more interesting when more information is given about nouns. For example, a noun phrase such as *the zombie* can be expanded by adding an adjective: *the <u>scary</u> zombie*. Prepositional phrases can follow a noun phrase to add information about time or place. For example: *the scary zombie <u>in the cave</u>*.

Behind the old shelter, Kim discovers something surprising. A turtle nest full of eggs! That is what Turpin was looking for.

1

Choose the best adjective from the box to complete the noun phrase in each sentence.

cosy	hard	safer	beautiful

a) Kim walked along a .... beach.

b) Kim saw a .... nest.

c) She decides to build the turtles a .... shelter.

d) She would have to use some .... wood.

2

Underline the noun phrase in each sentence.

a) She saw the cute, fragile turtle eggs.

b) They were in danger from deadly and aggressive mobs.

Luckily Kim has plenty of wood in her inventory and she begins crafting a fence that will surround the nest and create a safe path for the baby turtles into the water.

3

Draw lines to join each sentence opener on the left to the most suitable prepositional phrase on the right.

Kim felt the sturdy wood	sitting on the sand.
She was surely the best crafter	in her hand.
Kim stared at Turpin the turtle	somewhere nearby.
She knew there was danger	in the world.

4

Write two sentences about the beach, each with an expanded noun phrase (containing an adjective and a noun) followed by a prepositional phrase.

....

....

....

....

COLOUR IN HOW MANY EMERALDS YOU EARNED

31

FRONTED ADVERBIALS

When an adverbial (a word, phrase or clause that adds extra information to a verb) is used at the beginning of a sentence, it is known as a fronted adverbial. A fronted adverbial helps to describe the action that will follow. For example: _Slowly and carefully_, she moved across the sand. Fronted adverbials can also indicate time. For example: _After the storm_, she left the shelter.

Kim works fast but the sun is starting to set. Another drowned emerges from the ocean and begins to shuffle towards Turpin and the eggs.

 1

Underline the fronted adverbial in each sentence.

a) From the shelter, Kim could hear the enemy approaching.

b) When seeing the drowned, she prepared her sword.

c) After the fight, Kim had a rest in the old shelter.

d) During the night, she was worried about the turtles.

2

Kim thinks back over everything that has happened. Draw lines to join each fronted adverbial on the left to the best sentence ending on the right.

In the water,	it was safe and warm.
Beneath the sand,	she found some seagrass.
Inside the shelter,	Kim knew there was treasure.
During the fight,	she had feared for her life.

The next morning, Kim wakes early and runs outside to check on Turpin. The eggs have hatched and Turpin's baby turtles are using Kim's fences to find the sea.

3

Rewrite each sentence so that the adverbial phrase becomes a fronted adverbial.

a) Kim was eager to check on Turpin after resting.

....

b) She saw the baby turtles while walking along the beach.

....

c) Kim saw a shipwreck lying on the sand while looking around.

....

4

♥ Write two sentences, each with a fronted adverbial, giving more information about Kim's adventure on the beach.

a) ....

....

b) ....

....

COLOUR IN HOW MANY EMERALDS YOU EARNED

THE POSSESSIVE APOSTROPHE

A possessive apostrophe shows ownership – when something in a sentence belongs to someone or something else. For example: *the turtle's beach* – the apostrophe in *turtle's* suggests that the beach belongs to that turtle. If the beach belongs to more than one (plural) turtle (turtles), the apostrophe is written after the *s* – *the turtles' beach*.

Kim is so happy to see the baby turtles. They are cute and very curious. She watches as they explore their new home.

1

Add the possessive apostrophe to each of the **emboldened** words below.

*The shelter was safe and **Turpins** babies were having fun. She was very pleased*

*she had **Samis** spare sword with her. Those drowned were tough, but for Kim the*

__fights__ outcome was a happy one.

2

Underline each word requiring a possessive apostrophe in the passage below. Write the correctly punctuated words in the spaces provided.

There were so many baby turtles. The turtles nest was near to Kims shelter.

Zombies and creepers were distant worries as Kim looked for treasure and

shipwrecks near the waters edge.

Kim has to force herself to stop watching the turtles playing on the sand. She has treasure to find!

3

Write a sentence about each of the following. Include a possessive apostrophe in each of your sentences.

a) an explorer map belonging to Kim

b) a nest belonging to the turtles

c) the adventures belonging to Kim and Sami

4

Write two sentences: one containing an apostrophe showing singular possession and one containing an apostrophe showing plural possession.

a) Singular possession

b) Plural possession

DIRECT SPEECH

Direct speech is used to show the exact words a character is saying or has said. For example: <u>*Watch out for creepers,*</u> *warned Kim* – the underlined words are spoken by Kim. The spoken words begin with a capital letter and require inverted commas around them. The punctuation follows the spoken words: *"Watch out for creepers,"* *warned Kim*. The words *warned Kim* are known as a reporting clause, showing who is speaking. A reporting clause is usually separated from the spoken words by a comma, a question mark or an exclamation mark.

Kim pulls the explorer map out of her inventory to check where the buried treasure can be found. As she does so, she is surprised by a familiar voice. It is Sami!

I

Add inverted commas to the sentences below.

a) Welcome to the beach , smiled Kim .

b) I love your turtle enclosure , said Sami .

c) Kim said , There is buried treasure nearby .

d) Where do we need to dig ? asked Sami .

e) Kim laughed , Come on , I will show you .

The map shows that the treasure is buried beside the old shipwreck. As Kim and Sami approach it, more drowned come shuffling out of the ocean, ready to attack!

2

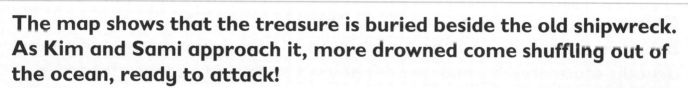

Add the missing punctuation to each of these sentences.

a) "Look out   "   screamed Kim

b) We have to fight together   "   yelled Sami.

c) Kim muttered   "I am sick of these annoying watery mobs   "

d) Sami gasped, "That was the last of them   Good fighting, Kim

3

Rewrite each of these sentences so that they have direct speech.

a) Kim told Sami that they should dig up the treasure.

....

b) Sami asked Kim if she had a shovel to help him dig.

....

c) Kim wondered if there were ruins under the sea.

....

COMMAS

Commas can be used to separate items in a list. They are placed between each item in a list apart from the final two items, which are usually separated by *and* or *or*. They also separate some clauses in sentences and are often placed after a fronted adverbial. Commas are also used in direct speech, for example after a reporting clause: *Kim asked, "Where are you going?"*

Nervous in case more drowned appear, Kim and Sami quickly get to work with their shovels on the spot that the explorer map shows them.

1

Draw lines to join each sentence to the correct description of the use of the comma.

Kim hoped to find ore, weapons and potions.	With direct speech
As quickly as possible, they dug up the sand.	After a fronted adverbial
The hole was deep, but there was no sign of treasure.	In a list
Suddenly Sami called out, "I've found it!"	To separate clauses

2

Insert commas in the correct places in the passage below.

Kim had been to many places including the jungle forest mountain and cave biomes. The beach was her favourite of all but she knew it had its dangers.

Excited and nervous, Sami opens the buried treasure chest.

3

Circle each comma which has been added incorrectly in the passage below.

The chest, was heavy and Sami hoped that meant it was, full of cool loot like jewels, weapons potions and tools. Sami, opened it up to see what was inside. Kim took out each item: a chainmail helmet, a gold ingot some TNT a sword and, a Potion of Water Breathing. Yes! They had found, it!

4

Rewrite the passage in question 3, removing incorrect commas. Add three commas where needed.

....

....

....

....

COLOUR IN HOW MANY EMERALDS YOU EARNED

39

TENSE

Tense tells us when something has happened, is happening or will happen. When an action has been completed by the present (i.e. by now), or was completed by a particular point in the past, it is known as the perfect tense. This uses the past or present form of the verb *to have* and the past participle of the main verb (e.g. walk<u>ed</u>). For example, *Kim <u>had</u> walked a long way* uses the past form of *to have* and *Kim <u>has</u> walked a long way* uses the present form of *to have*.

The Potion of Water Breathing will help Kim stay underwater longer when she explores the ocean. What about Sami? He has brought a potion of his own. They are all set to explore the deep!

1

Choose the correct form of the verb **to have** to complete each sentence.

a) Sami .... brewed his own potion before

setting off. (past)

b) Kim .... fought many mobs on her

adventure so far. (present)

2

Tick the two sentences which are written correctly.

The potion had been buried. ☐

Turtles has been born on the beach. ☐

Kim and Sami has found a buried treasure chest. ☐

They have seen some great places. ☐

COLOUR IN HOW MANY
EMERALDS YOU EARNED ◇◇◇◇

ADVENTURE ROUND-UP

LOOKING OUT TO SEA

Kim and Sami look out at the deep, blue sea in front of them. It looks very mysterious and inviting. There will be new and dangerous enemies to face, but lots of cool, friendly creatures and exciting items to find as well.

LET'S GET WET!

Always ready for a new adventure, Kim and Sami wade into the water together and begin to swim…

COMPOSITION

WATERY WORLD

You may think you are a top explorer if you have visited all the land biomes and encountered all the mobs that live there, but there is a whole new world to discover under the waves. From sunken ruins to playful dolphins and squishy squid, you are guaranteed to find something interesting when you take the plunge!

DIVING IN

With their potions ready, Sami and Kim are ready to head out into the ocean to see what they can discover...

AUDIENCE AND PURPOSE

When writing a text, it is important to think about who it is being written for – the audience – and why it is being written – the purpose. Is the piece of writing aimed at an adult or a child? Is it being written to inform (usually non-fiction) or to entertain (usually fiction)?

Sami and Kim wade into the water until their feet no longer reach the sandy floor. As they swim, they see squid beneath them.

Imagine writing books based on Sami and Kim's adventure. Draw lines to join each book title to the intended audience.

Book title	A Simple Guide to the Ocean	A Technical Guide to Ocean Biomes	Exploring Oceans with your Kids

Audience	Adults	Younger children	Teenagers

2

Draw lines to join each sentence to its purpose.

Sentence   **Purpose**

The serene squid made a funny, gloopy
noise as it swam.

to inform

Squid are a passive aquatic mob.

Squid ink sacs can be used to craft black dye.

to entertain

Strange plants swayed beneath the
shimmering water.

PARAGRAPHS

Paragraphs are important because they help writing to be easier to read and understand. Groups of sentences about different things can be organised into paragraphs. For example, a group of sentences about a setting could be one paragraph, and a group of sentences about a character could be another.

They could swim underwater for a short time, but Sami and Kim know they should save their Potions of Water Breathing for when they find something worth exploring.

 I

Draw lines to join each paragraph of text to the correct description of it.

Paragraph	Description
All around was blue water. It looked beautiful but there were dangers beneath the surface.	About a character's feelings
The explorer had strong arms and carried various weapons. Scars on her hands and face showed she had been in many battles.	About a setting
Slowly, it dragged itself out of the water. Creepy and deadly, it started to approach.	About a character's appearance
Cautiously, she stepped into the water. She thought she was brave, but she was also nervous.	About a creature

Kim spots a shipwreck on the seabed below and wants to check it out. Sami is not so sure.

2

Label each sentence below as paragraph 1 (which describes a setting) or paragraph 2 (which describes a problem). Write P1 or P2 at the end of each sentence to show if the sentence is from paragraph 1 (P1) or paragraph 2 (P2).

a)   They knew there could be dangerous mobs down there.

b)   They could see the front of the ship had broken away.

c)   Sami wondered if they could hold their breath that long.

d)   It appeared to have once been an amazing vessel.

3

Write two paragraphs of three sentences each. One paragraph should describe the shipwreck and the other paragraph should describe a problem Sami and Kim might face there.

....

....

....

....

....

....

ORGANISING NON-FICTION WRITING

Non-fiction texts have a number of organisational features (such as tables and diagrams to present information, photographs and other images) and carefully considered headings and subheadings for paragraphs and groups of paragraphs.

Sami is worried about encountering drowned on the ocean floor. Kim knows all about these mobs though.

 l

Match each piece of information on the left to the most suitable subheading it could be found under in a book about the ocean biome.

Information	Subheading
Drowned are the most common enemy.	Introduction
The biome is mostly water.	Water Creatures
Dolphins and squid are not uncommon.	Hostile Mobs

2

Another subheading is 'Drowned'. Write at least two sentences which could appear under this subheading.

....

....

....

....

Kim tells Sami everything she knows about drowned.

3

Think of a suitable subheading for each paragraph that is described below.

a) All about different places to visit and explore.

What each world is like and what it is called.

b) Information about the groups who do not attack,
such as chicken, salmon, squid, turtles and villagers.

c) About how to find different ores.

4

Write a paragraph of at least three sentences to describe the ocean biome.
Make sure each sentence includes at least one fact about the biome. Check
that each sentence makes sense by saying it aloud before you write.

Ocean Biome

ORGANISING FICTION WRITING

Fiction writing needs careful organisation so that it makes sense to the reader. Characters and settings need describing. New paragraphs should be used for different events and ideas. It is vital that events are well-written and in an order that the reader can understand.

Sami decides to swim down to the shipwreck and see what he can find.

Draw lines to join each piece of text on the left to the story part it comes from.

Text

Story part

Sami was a strong swimmer. He was strong, athletic and full of confidence. He thought he could reach the wreck and get back safely without running out of breath.

He quickly swam back up with his loot. His lungs ached and he took a grateful gulp of air at the surface. His dive for treasure had been a great success.

The ancient shipwreck was lodged in the sand beneath the clear blue waves.

He searched the wreck until almost all his breath was gone. He was now in danger and had to search frantically. Eventually, just before he had to give up, he found an old chest.

Beginning – setting description

Beginning – character description

Middle – tackling a problem

End

Sami and Kim keep swimming as they look down into the watery depths for interesting things. Suddenly, a pod of dolphins appears and they leap out of the water.

2

Think of one sentence that you might include in each part of a story about a dolphin in the ocean biome. Say your sentence aloud to ensure it makes sense.

a) Beginning – setting description

b) Beginning – character description

c) Middle – tackling a problem

d) End

WRITING ABOUT CHARACTERS

Characters need to be described well so that the reader can get a good understanding of them. Describing a character as 'mean' gives a very different idea to saying they are a 'kind' person. Consider what the character looks like and their characteristics (for example, are they weak or strong, brave or cowardly, fast or slow?) You should also try to show how the character is feeling.

The dolphins swim and jump around Sami and Kim. They want to play!

 1

Draw lines to join each sentence to what it is telling the reader about a character. Here the character being described is a dolphin.

Sentence	What it tells about the character
The dolphin's sleek body rippled through the water.	How the character feels
The dolphin was excited to find two people to play with.	How the character looks
By swimming alongside Sami and Kim, the helpful dolphin gave them a speed boost!	How the character behaves

2

Good adjectives are very important in description. Look at each part of the character descriptions in question 1. Find and copy the adjective used in each.

....

Sami and Kim have a great time playing and swimming with the dolphins. They wish they had another friend with them to share the fun.

3

Think of a new character who could accompany Sami and Kim. Write key words for each aspect of their character.

a) What does the character look like (three adjectives)?

b) How does the character move (three adverbs)?

c) How do they feel about going on an adventure (three adjectives)?

4

Write a short paragraph of three sentences describing the character you have started to think about in question 3.

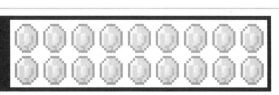

COLOUR IN HOW MANY
EMERALDS YOU EARNED

WRITING ABOUT SETTINGS

When writing about setting, it is important to use good description to enable the reader to imagine the place in the same way as you. Careful description can help the setting to come alive and help the reader to feel like they can really see it.

Sami and Kim follow the dolphins as they swim further out to sea. They are far from land now. Deep below, on the bottom of the ocean, Sami spots an underwater ruin.

1

Think about the underwater ruin and how it might look. Write six adjectives to describe it.

....

....

2

Answer the questions below about the ruin. Use your adjectives from above to help you.

a) What can you see? ....

....

b) What can you hear? ....

....

c) How does it feel to be there? ....

....

Sami and Kim take a deep breath and dive down to the ruin. If they find something interesting, they will use their potions to stay down there longer and explore.

3

Put together the ideas from questions 1 and 2 to write a short paragraph (of three or four sentences) describing the underwater ruin.

4

Think of another biome (it could be one you make up) and think of three adjectives to describe it. Then think of, and say aloud, a short paragraph (of three sentences) to describe that setting. Write down this setting description.

Adjectives:

Description:

COLOUR IN HOW MANY EMERALDS YOU EARNED

PROOFREADING

Before your writing is ready for somebody else to read, it needs to go through the important process of proofreading. This means carefully checking for mistakes in spelling and punctuation to ensure that the sentences make sense and are clear to understand.

Sami and Kim explore the ruin. Some of the walls are made of stylish sandstone. Sami also finds a treasure chest!

1

Underline the three spelling and punctuation errors in each sentence below. Then rewrite each sentence correctly.

a) Kim watched as sami starrted to mine the sandstone with his pickaxe

....

b) The sandstone had been, carved with pritty pattuns.

....

c) It was one of the most beoutiful things kim had ever scene.

....

d) Sami thort to himself, "This is the luckyest discovery ever!

Sami is looting armour and golden apples from the chest and doesn't notice some drowned among the ruins. How can Kim warn him?

2

Underline the eight spelling and punctuation mistakes in the passage below. Rewrite the passage with these mistakes corrected.

Kim swam over, to Sami and got his attenshun She pointed at the drowned. They had spotted them and were moving to attak. They could not hold their breth long enough to fight the mobs, so they quickly started swimming back up to the surface? "That was close!" gasped Sami as they poked there heads above the waives.

3

Read the sentence below. Explain what stops it from making sense.

Kim knew where they were so she had been here before.

EDITING

Editing a text can help to improve it. Making changes to grammar and vocabulary can help the sentences to be clearer and more effective. Some words might be changed for more interesting or exciting vocabulary.

Sami and Kim are very far out into the ocean but have still not used their Potions of Water Breathing. The ocean is very deep here. What might be lurking in these dark depths?

 1

Read each piece of text below. Rewrite them using pronouns and better vocabulary to replace the highlighted words.

a) Kim looked at the *big* ocean. *Kim* thought it looked *nice*.

....

b) Sami had found a *good* sea lantern. *The sea lantern* looked *sparkly*.

....

2

♥ Kim is in the underwater ruin and a drowned is about to attack. Read the passage below about it. Change the order of the sentences and make improvements to the vocabulary and grammar to make it easier and better to read.

It were a nice day and Kim was in the nice blue ocean. Kim checked she had her sword, a drowned was coming. The drowned was not nice. Kim saw a drowned.

....

....

....

....

COLOUR IN HOW MANY EMERALDS YOU EARNED

ADVENTURE ROUND-UP

DANGERS OF THE DEEP

The idea of swimming into the deep ocean is scary but exciting. There are many more dangers down there but also the chance of finding monuments and rare items.

OCEAN POTIONS

Sami and Kim still have their Potions of Water Breathing. They have come this far. It would be crazy to turn back now. It is time to go deeper than they have ever gone before in search of adventure!

CREATIVE WRITING

IN THE DEEP

If you are out at sea, just keep going and sooner or later you will find a deep ocean biome. You can tell the water is deep because it is darker at the surface, and the seabed will be made of gravel and covered in kelp.

DIVING DOWN

In the deep ocean, you may also find an ocean monument to explore but be very careful. Elder guardians are known to prowl their waterlogged corridors!

DEEP-SEA EXPLORATION

Having reached the deep ocean, Kim and Sami bob in the water as they decide what to do next. Kim wants to find an ocean monument, so Sami comes up with a plan to craft a conduit. That will refill their oxygen and also help to protect them from enemy mobs. They will need a lot of nautilus shells and a heart of the sea – some very rare items. The quest is on!

PLANNING 1

All writing must be planned carefully. Before you write a sentence, think about it and say it aloud. For a longer piece of writing, make a plan of what will happen in different parts of it and think about the order of events. Planning also involves thinking about key words and ideas.

The first thing Sami and Kim need to do is find lots of nautilus shells. Sometimes drowned drop those, so it is time to get fighting.

Draw lines to join each piece of text to the appropriate story part.

| They saw some drowned on the ocean floor and battled them. | They defeated the drowned and earned some shells, but not enough. | Kim and Sami dived into the water, looking for drowned. |

| Beginning | Middle | End |

Write an idea you might include if you were writing information under each of these subheadings.

a) Beach Biome ....

....

b) Deep Ocean Biome ....

....

PLANNING 2

All writing should aim to be interesting for the reader. Whether it is a simple story for three-year-olds or a complicated non-fiction text for an adult, it must be planned to include ideas and information that the audience will want to hear or find out about. This all needs careful planning and thinking about the ideas to include.

If Sami and Kim are going to craft a conduit, they will need a lot more nautilus shells. Luckily Sami and Kim know all about drowned and where to find them.

1

Shade in the four boxes which contain an idea that would be **unsuitable** for a book about mobs.

villagers	zombies	creepers	beetroot	ore

spiders	mining	cows	shipwrecks	drowned

2

Read the ideas below for a story about Sami in the deep ocean. Which would you be most likely to include? Tick two.

Sea creatures ☐

Sami's favourite food ☐

Sami's farming abilities ☐

Sami's swimming skills ☐

Sami and Kim decide to split up to try to find more drowned to battle with. They each drink their Potion of Water Breathing to stay underwater for longer.

3

Which of these ideas would you be most likely to include in a story about Kim in the deep ocean? Tick three.

The scene is described with lots of detail about the ocean Kim can see – a nearby shipwreck and dolphins.

Kim discovers an underwater ruin, but danger is not far away as drowned start to approach.

Kim reaches the top of the mountain. She can see the village where she will find shelter and food.

Kim wonders if the enemies will drop more nautilus shells, and worries that she will run out of breath.

4

Write three subheadings you might use in a book about the deep ocean.

....

....

....

STORY WRITING 1

In order to plan a good story, you should think about who the characters are and what they are like, what the setting is like, and the plot (what is going to happen in the story). Stories often have a problem – something that the characters have to solve or overcome – as this creates interest and excitement.

Sami sees some drowned on the bottom of the ocean. He takes a deep breath and swims down to fight them.

1

Think about the main character for a story of your choice. Write two sentences to briefly describe the character and two more to describe the setting.

....

....

....

....

2

Start to think more about the character and the story plot by answering the questions below.

a) What is the character's mission? ....

....

b) How does the character feel? ....

....

c) How has the character prepared for their mission? ....

....

Sami battles against the drowned but it is hard to hold his breath for this long. The potion will wear off soon.

3

What problems might your character encounter on their mission? It would be boring for the reader if nothing happened, so think about a challenge they face such as tough conditions, hostile mobs or maybe even both.

Think of two problems your character might face and about how they might feel.

Problem	How the character feels

4

Choose one of your ideas from question 3. Write a paragraph which makes it clear to the reader that there is a problem. Describe the problem and how your character feels. Remember to say your sentences aloud before writing them.

....

....

....

....

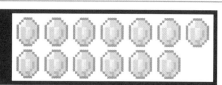

COLOUR IN HOW MANY EMERALDS YOU EARNED

STORY WRITING 2

Telling the reader about a problem (and how the character deals with it) allows you to write lots of exciting things. Think about the dangers faced – how scary is it and how does your character survive? Once the problem has been overcome, the story can move on towards the ending, which will say whether the character completed their mission.

Sami hopes the drowned he is defeating will drop enough nautilus shells for their crafting.

1

Consider the problem you have described on page 63. Put ideas into the table to help you plan how your character overcomes the problem.

What are the dangers?	What does the character need? (e.g. weapons)	What key things happen in resolving the problem?

2

Use your ideas from question 1 to write a paragraph telling the story of how the problem was resolved. Say your sentences aloud, write them, then check them.

....

....

....

....

Sami swims back to the surface after the long and difficult battle. He is almost out of breath.

3

Consider your story ending. Add notes to this table to help you plan some ideas.

What happens?	Was the mission a success?	How does the character feel?

4

Write your story ending using your notes from question 3. Remember to say your sentences aloud before writing them.

....

....

....

....

COLOUR IN HOW MANY
EMERALDS YOU EARNED

NON-FICTION WRITING 1

Non-fiction writing should be clear and concise – this means writing the key details without adding any unnecessary information that could cause confusion. Information is often clearer when written under subheadings that give an idea about what each section is about. Saying sentences aloud before writing helps to make sure they just contain the key details.

Sami and Kim meet up, treading water on the ocean's surface. They have collected enough nautilus shells! Now they need a heart of the sea from a buried treasure chest. Kim knows an aquatic mob that can help them.

 1

Imagine that you are writing a book for adventurers, starting with an introduction giving general information about mobs. Write ideas for this introduction in the table below.

What are mobs?	What types are there?

2

Write an introduction using your notes from question 1 to help you.

....

....

....

....

If Sami and Kim feed a dolphin with some fish, it will lead them to a useful location. It could be buried treasure!

3

Choose three mobs and give more detail about each. Write the key ideas for what you will say about them.

Mob 1:	Mob 2:	Mob 3:

4

Use your notes from question 3 to write a subheading (the mob name) and a short description of each mob.

Mob 1:

Mob 2:

Mob 3:

NON-FICTION WRITING 2

Non-fiction writing will often include some information in greater detail. In order to do this, you need to use more facts and have a good understanding about what you are writing about.

Sami feeds some cod to a passing dolphin and they swim after it as it zooms off.

 1

Write down ideas for everything you know about dolphins in order to prepare for writing in greater detail about them.

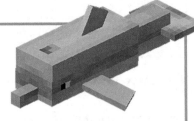

Dolphins

2

Use your ideas from question 1 to write a paragraph about dolphins. Remember to say your sentences aloud before writing them.

The dolphin leads Sami and Kim to buried treasure. Inside they find a heart of the sea and some armour. Those will be useful!

3

You are also going to explain the dangers faced in the deep ocean. This section will begin with information about health and hostile mobs. Plan this section by answering the questions below.

a) What is health? ....

How is it lost? ....

b) What are hostile mobs? ....

What can they do to a character? ....

4

Use your answers in question 3 to write two short paragraphs about Minecraft dangers under the subheadings of 'Health' and 'Hostile Mobs'.

Health

....

....

....

Hostile Mobs

....

....

....

COLOUR IN HOW MANY EMERALDS YOU EARNED

EDITING

::

Editing involves reviewing your writing and trying to improve the grammar and vocabulary you have used.

Sami uses the nautilus shells and the heart of the sea to craft a conduit. This amazing cube would protect them as they explore an ocean monument.

I

Edit each pair of sentences below, changing the underlined words for more interesting vocabulary. You could also try joining the sentences together and adding extra adjectives or adverbs. For example:

Original: *It was a <u>nice</u> day. Kim was <u>happy</u> to be going on an adventure.*

Edited: *It was a glorious day and Kim was excited to be starting an awesome adventure.*

a) **Original:** They swam down to the <u>old</u> monument. Kim was excited.

   Edited: ....

   ....

b) **Original:** They <u>went into</u> the monument. They knew it was dangerous.

   Edited: ....

   ....

c) **Original:** Suddenly, <u>something was there</u>. It was an elder guardian.

   Edited: ....

   ....

The elder guardian attacks Sami and Kim, shooting a deadly laser beam from its eye. The conduit damages the elder guardian as Sami and Kim battle with their swords.

2

Choose one of your own pieces of story writing – from page 63 question 4, or page 64 question 2 – and read and edit it. Think about any words you could improve or add and any sentences you could change. Give up to four examples of changes you have made below.

3

Choose one of your own pieces of non-fiction writing – from page 66 question 2, or page 68 question 2 – and read and edit it. Think about any words or sentences you could change, and whether all the information makes sense. Give up to four examples of changes you have made below.

PROOFREADING

Proofreading helps you to check for any spelling mistakes and missing punctuation in your writing. This will improve it and make it easier to read.

With the conduit power pulsing through the water, Sami and Kim defeat the elder guardian. They have faced the deadliest enemy in the ocean and survived, thanks to their careful planning.

1

Read through the paragraphs you have written for question 4 on page 69. List three mistakes you can find and correct (use a dictionary or ask an adult to help you check spellings). If you have fewer than three mistakes, write down things you were looking for when proofreading.

....

....

....

2

Read through your answer to question 4 on page 65. List three mistakes you can find and correct. If you have fewer than three mistakes, choose some words from your writing and think of even better words to use instead.

....

....

....

COLOUR IN HOW MANY EMERALDS YOU EARNED

ADVENTURE ROUND-UP

SEA TO SHORE

Sami and Kim swim back to the surface, exhausted but thrilled by their deep ocean adventure. It will be a long swim back to shore, and then an even longer walk home after that.

RICH REWARDS

All that effort was absolutely worth it. They have inventories full of rare and useful items, as well as another incredible story to tell around the campfire.

ANSWERS

::

Page 5

1 **il**legal   **im**perfect
indefinite   **ir**regular   [1 emerald each]

2 **a)** irresponsible   **b)** impossible
   c) illegible   **d)** incorrect   [1 emerald each]

Pages 6–7

1 furni**ture**   trea**sure**
mea**sure**   adven**ture**   [1 emerald each]

2 **a)** creature   **b)** adventure
   c) nature   **d)** treasure   [1 emerald each]

3 **a)** enclo**sure**   **b)** plea**sure**
   c) struc**ture**   **d)** pic**ture**   [1 emerald each]

4 **a)** The definition should acknowledge that 'capture' means to take something into one's possession. **Example sentence:** Kim might capture a creature to take home.   [1 emerald for the definition; 1 emerald for a correct sentence]

   b) The definition should acknowledge that 'leisure' means spare time or relaxing. **Example sentence:** Kim will have plenty of leisure time once her adventure is over.   [1 emerald for the definition; 1 emerald for a correct sentence]

Pages 8–9

1 **a)** confusion   **b)** television
   c) revision   **d)** exclusion   [1 emerald each]

2 **a)** decision   **b)** confusion
   c) occasion   **d)** vision   [1 emerald each]

3 **a)** include   **b)** conclude
   c) provide   **d)** erode   [1 emerald each]

4 **a)** explode   **b)** intrude
   c) revise   **d)** evade   [1 emerald each]

Pages 10–11

1 Boxes joined as follows:

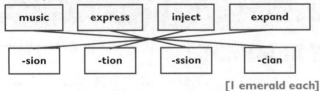

[1 emerald each]

2 **a)** mathematician   **b)** action   **c)** hesitation
                                    [1 emerald each]

3 **a)** permit   **b)** act
   c) magic   **d)** comprehend   [1 emerald each]

4 Ensure each sentence makes sense and uses the chosen form of the given word correctly. **Example sentences:**
   a) Something on the map caught her attention.
                                     [1 emerald]

   b) She intended to find out exactly what it was.
                                     [1 emerald]

Pages 12–13

1 **a)** noti**c**ed   **b)** de**c**ide   **c)** **c**entre
                                    [1 emerald each]

2 **a)** g**u**ide   **b)** b**u**ild
   c) tong**ue**   **d)** g**u**ilty   [1 emerald each]

3 **a)** laugh   **b)** taught   **c)** caught
                                    [1 emerald each]

4 **a)** The answer should acknowledge that the short 'i' sound uses a 'u' in each word.   [1 emerald]

   b) **Example sentence:** She was busy mining redstone.   [1 emerald]

Pages 14–15

1 Sami   shelter   spider   structure
                                    [1 emerald each]

2 **a)** an enemy or opponent   [1 emerald]
   b) the leaves of a plant (or tree)   [1 emerald]

3 **a)** scene   seen   [1 emerald]
   b) mail   male   [1 emerald]
   c) meat   meet   [1 emerald]
   d) groan   grown   [1 emerald]

4 Each word to be used correctly in a sentence. **Examples:**
   a) She decided to accept that she was lost.
                                     [1 emerald]
     There was nothing except sand at the beach.
                                     [1 emerald]
   b) The bright sun began to affect her eyes.   [1 emerald]
     She began to feel the effect of a long walk.
                                     [1 emerald]

Pages 16–17

1 **a)** s**y**mbol   **b)** Eg**y**pt   **c)** g**y**m
   d) c**y**gnet   **e)** rh**y**thm   **f)** h**y**mn
                                    [1 emerald each]

2 **a)** mysterious   **b)** oxygen   **c)** myth
                                    [1 emerald each]

3 Lyly – Lily   gimnast – gymnast
tipical – typical   cristal – crystal   [1 emerald each]

4 Sentences will vary but must contain the given word used correctly. **Examples:**
   a) It was a mystery where the noise came from.
                                     [1 emerald]
   b) There was a special symbol on the treasure chest.
                                     [1 emerald]
   c) Kim had heard a strange myth about the forest.
                                     [1 emerald]

Pages 18–20

1 echoed   scheme   [1 emerald each]

2 chef – someone who prepares and cooks food
machine – something mechanical designed to do a job
[1 emerald for each word;
1 emerald for any suitable definition]

3 a) unique   b) technique
  c) league   d) fatigue   [1 emerald each]

4 a) an old object (noun) or high in value because of
    its old age (adjective)   [1 emerald]
  b) uncertain or indefinite   [1 emerald]

5 scent   scenery   fascinating
[1 emerald each]

6 Sentences will vary but must use the given words
correctly. **Example:**
Kim decided to ascend the tree. When she had seen
the view, she decided to descend the tree.
[1 emerald for the correct use of each word]

Page 23

1 Boxes joined as follows:

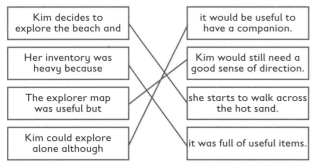

[1 emerald each]

2 Answers will vary. Ensure the conjunctions are used
correctly. **Examples:**
  a) The beach was sandy **and the sand was
    very hot**.   [1 emerald]
  b) Kim thought it looked beautiful **because it was
    a golden colour**.   [1 emerald]

Pages 24–25

1 "Good morning turtle. I am Kim."   [1 emerald]
2 Kim were walking along beach.   NS [1 emerald]
  Kim was walking along the beach.   S [1 emerald]
  Kim was walking on beach.   NS [1 emerald]
3 Answers will vary. Ensure each sentence is
grammatically correct. **Examples:**
  a) Turpin wanted to swim in the sea.   [1 emerald]
  b) What is it looking at?   [1 emerald]
  c) The beach is really good.   [1 emerald]
  d) There is a lot of sand.   [1 emerald]
4 Answers will vary. Ensure each sentence is
grammatically correct. **Example:**
The journey was very good. I expect I will have to
fight something soon, though. I think I will find a lot
of very exciting treasure. [1 emerald for each sentence]

Pages 26–27

1 a) a   b) a
  c) an   d) an   [1 emerald each]
2 an blue sky (a or the)   an seagrass (a or the)
  a sand (the or some)   an shipwreck (a)
  a underwater (an)   a ocean (the) [1 emerald each]
3 a) a (or the)   b) some
  c) The   d) Kim's   [1 emerald each]
4 Answers will vary. Ensure each sentence uses the
given determiner correctly. **Examples:**
  a) Kim should have known **those** drowned would
    come.   [1 emerald]
  b) It was a good job she saw **that** drowned
    behind her.   [1 emerald]
  c) She would learn from **this** mistake.   [1 emerald]
  d) **Every** adventure had danger.   [1 emerald]

Pages 28–29

1 a) it   b) she   c) it   d) they   [1 emerald each]
2 Kim – she
  the beach – it
  their shelter – theirs
  the person – they   [1 emerald each]
3 a) hers   b) theirs
  c) yours   d) ours   [1 emerald each]
4 Answers will vary. Each must be suitable. **Examples:**
  a) This adventure is mine.   [1 emerald]
  b) She decided that it was time to leave. [1 emerald]
  c) Nobody could see them inside the shelter.
        [1 emerald]

Pages 30–31

1 a) beautiful   b) cosy
  c) safer   d) hard   [1 emerald each]
2 a) the cute, fragile turtle eggs   [1 emerald]
  b) deadly and aggressive mobs   [1 emerald]
3 Boxes joined as follows:

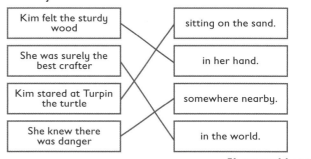

[1 emerald each]

4 Answers will vary. Each must contain an expanded
noun phrase followed by a prepositional phrase.
Examples:
Kim could feel gritty, rough sand in her boots.

[2 emeralds]

The funny and cute turtle slept in its new shelter.

[2 emeralds]

Pages 32–33

1. a) From the shelter   [I emerald]
    b) When seeing the drowned   [I emerald]
    c) After the fight   [I emerald]
    d) During the night   [I emerald]

2. Boxes joined as follows:

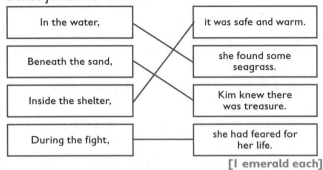

[I emerald each]

3. a) After resting, Kim was eager to check on Turpin. [I emerald]
    b) While walking along the beach, she saw the baby turtles. [I emerald]
    c) While looking around, Kim saw a shipwreck lying on the sand. [I emerald]

4. Answers will vary but each sentence must have a fronted adverbial. **Examples:**
    While looking out to sea, Kim saw something strange. [I emerald]

    As the wind blew the sand, Kim watched the waves on the shore. [I emerald]

Pages 34–35

1. Turpin's   Sami's   fight's
    [I emerald each]
2. turtles – turtles'   Kims – Kim's   waters – water's
    [I emerald each]
3. Answers will vary but each sentence must use the given information and a possessive apostrophe. **Examples:**
    a) Kim's explorer map was very useful.   [I emerald]
    b) It was warm in the turtles' nest.   [I emerald]
    c) Kim and Sami's adventures were the best.
    [I emerald]
4. Answers will vary. **Examples:**
    a) Kim's top is green and white.   [I emerald]
    b) The creatures' home was well protected.
    [I emerald]

Pages 36–37

1. a) "Welcome to the beach," smiled Kim. [I emerald]
    b) "I love your turtle enclosure," said Sami. [I emerald]
    c) Kim said, "There is buried treasure nearby."
    [I emerald]
    d) "Where do we need to dig?" asked Sami. [I emerald]
    e) Kim laughed, "Come on, I will show you."
    [I emerald]

2. Answers will vary. **Examples:**
    a) "Look out!" screamed Kim.   [I emerald]
    b) "We have to fight together!" yelled Sami.
    [I emerald]
    c) Kim muttered, "I am sick of these annoying watery mobs." [I emerald]
    d) Sami gasped, "That was the last of them. Good fighting, Kim!" [I emerald]
3. Answers will vary. **Examples:**
    a) "We should dig up the treasure," Kim told Sami.
    [I emerald]
    b) "Do you have a shovel, Kim?" asked Sami.
    [I emerald]
    c) "Are there ruins under the sea?" wondered Kim.
    [I emerald]

Pages 38–39

1. Boxes joined as follows:

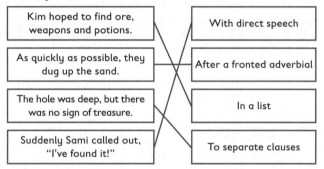

[I emerald each]

2. Kim had been to many places including the jungle, forest, mountain and cave biomes. The beach was her favourite of all, but she knew it had its dangers.
    [I emerald each]

3. The chest⌒ was heavy and Sami hoped that meant it was⌒ full of cool loot like jewels, weapons potions and tools. Sami⌒ opened it up to see what was inside. Kim took out each item: a chainmail helmet, a gold ingot some TNT a sword and⌒ a Potion of Water Breathing. Yes! They had found⌒ it! [I emerald each]

4. The chest was heavy and Sami hoped that meant it was full of cool loot like jewels, weapons, potions and tools. Sami opened it up to see what was inside. Kim took out each item: a chainmail helmet, a gold ingot, some TNT, a sword and a Potion of Water Breathing. Yes! They had found it!
    [I emerald for each correctly added comma]

Page 40

1. a) had   b) has   [I emerald each]
2. The potion had been buried.   [I emerald]
    They have seen some great places.   [I emerald]

Page 43

1 Boxes joined as follows:

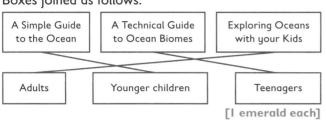

[1 emerald each]

2 Boxes joined as follows:

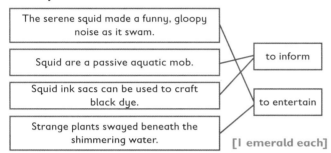

[1 emerald each]

Pages 44–45

1 Boxes joined as follows:

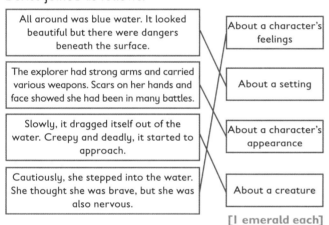

[1 emerald each]

2 a) P2   b) P1
   c) P2   d) P1   [1 emerald each]

3 Answers will vary. Ensure that one paragraph describes the shipwreck, and one paragraph describes a problem they face. [1 emerald for each paragraph]

Pages 46–47

1 Boxes joined as follows:

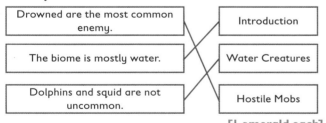

[1 emerald each]

2 Each sentence in the paragraph should be correctly constructed and initially said aloud. Each should relate to the given subject. [1 emerald for each sentence up to a maximum of 2]

3 Answers will vary. Ensure that each given answer is appropriate. **Examples:**
   a) Biomes (or Minecraft Worlds) [1 emerald]
   b) Passive Mobs (or Friendly Mobs) [1 emerald]
   c) Mining (or Searching for Ores) [1 emerald]

4 Each sentence in the paragraph should be correctly constructed and initially said aloud. Each should relate to the ocean biome. [1 emerald for each sentence up to a maximum of 3]

Pages 48–49

1 Boxes joined as follows:

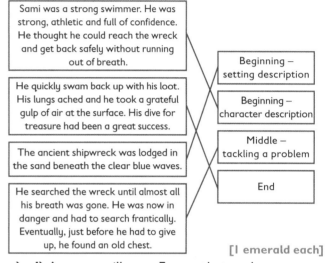

[1 emerald each]

2 a)–d) Answers will vary. Ensure that each sentence relates to the relevant story part. [1 emerald each]

Pages 50–51

1 Boxes joined as follows:

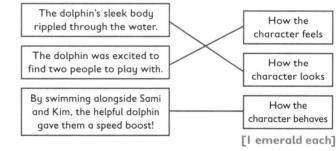

[1 emerald each]

2 sleek   excited   helpful [1 emerald each]

3 Answers will vary. **Examples:**
   a) tall, short, strong [1 emerald each]
   b) quickly, slowly, awkwardly [1 emerald each]
   c) excited, happy, nervous [1 emerald each]

4 Each sentence in the paragraph should be correctly constructed and initially said aloud. Each should relate to the description of the character. [1 emerald for each sentence]

Pages 52–53

1 Answers will vary. **Examples:**

ancient	amazing	incredible
old	interesting	spooky

[1 emerald each]

2 a)–c) Answers will vary. Ensure that each sentence relates to the given prompt.

[1 emerald for each sentence]

3 Each sentence in the paragraph should be correctly constructed and initially said aloud. Each should relate to the underwater ruin. [1 emerald for each sentence up to a maximum of 3]

4 Answers will vary. [1 emerald for each adjective; 1 emerald for each sentence]

Pages 54–55

1 a) Kim watched as <u>sami</u> (*Sami*) <u>starrted</u> (*started*) to mine the sandstone with his pickaxe<u>.</u> (*add full stop*)
   b) The sandstone had been<u>,</u> (*remove comma*) carved with <u>pritty</u> (*pretty*) <u>pattuns</u> (*patterns*).
   c) It was one of the most <u>beoutiful</u> (*beautiful*) things <u>kim</u> (*Kim*) had ever <u>scene</u> (*seen*).
   d) Sami <u>thort</u> (*thought*) to himself, "This is the <u>luckyest</u> (*luckiest*) discovery ever<u>!</u> (*add speech marks*)

[1 emerald for each corrected mistake]

2 Kim swam over<u>,</u> (*remove comma*) to Sami and got his <u>attenshun</u> (*attention*)<u>_</u> (*add full stop*) She pointed at the drowned. They had spotted them and were moving to <u>attak</u> (*attack*). They could not hold their <u>breth</u> (*breath*) long enough to fight the mobs, so they quickly started swimming back up to the surface<u>?</u> (*replace question mark with full stop*) "That was close!" gasped Sami as they poked <u>there</u> (*their*) heads above the <u>waives</u> (*waves*).

[1 emerald for each corrected mistake]

3 The answer should acknowledge that the conjunction 'so' should be replaced by 'because' or 'as'. [1 emerald]

Page 56

1 Adjectives in the answers will vary. **Examples:**
   a) Kim looked at the <u>vast</u> ocean. <u>She</u> thought it looked <u>incredible</u>. [1 emerald for each word]
   b) Sami had found a <u>fantastic</u> sea lantern. <u>It</u> looked <u>beautiful</u>. [1 emerald for each word]

2 Answers will vary but the paragraph must make sense. **Example:**
   It was a wonderful day and Kim was swimming in the glorious, blue ocean. Suddenly, she saw a drowned. It was very unpleasant and was coming towards her. She checked that she had her sword.

[1 emerald for each sentence]

Page 59

1 Boxes joined as follows:

They saw some drowned on the ocean floor and battled them.	They defeated the drowned and earned some shells, but not enough.	Kim and Sami dived into the water, looking for drowned.
Beginning	Middle	End

[1 emerald each]

2 Answers will vary but must relate to the given biome. **Examples:**
   a) About the sand and what lives there, such as turtles. [1 emerald]
   b) About what might be found there, such as old monuments. [1 emerald]

Pages 60–61

1

plains	ore
mining	shipwrecks

[1 emerald each]

2 Sea creatures   Sami's swimming skills

[1 emerald each]

3 The scene is described… ✓ [1 emerald]
   Kim discovers an underwater ruin… ✓ [1 emerald]
   Kim wonders if the enemies… ✓ [1 emerald]

4 Answers will vary but must relate to the deep ocean biome. **Examples:**
   Deep Ocean Mobs
   Underwater Ruins
   Nautilus Shells [1 emerald each]

Pages 62–63

1 Answers will vary. Check that they are suitable for the setting and character. [1 emerald for each sentence]

2 a)–c) Answers will vary. Ensure that there is a coherent story idea. [1 emerald each]

3 Answers will vary. Ensure that the ideas fit in with the general story idea, and the character.

[1 mark for each completed section of the table]

4 Answers will vary. Each sentence in the paragraph should be correctly constructed and initially said aloud.

[1 emerald for describing the problem; 1 emerald for describing the character's feelings]

Pages 64–65

1 Answers will vary. Ensure the ideas make sense.

[1 emerald for each section]

2 Each sentence in the paragraph should be correctly constructed and initially said aloud. The content should include what the dangers are, what the characters need, and what happens.

[1 emerald for each of these ideas]

3 Answers will vary. Ensure the ideas make sense.

[1 emerald for each section]

4 Each sentence in the paragraph should be correctly constructed and initially said aloud. The content should include what happens, whether the mission was a success, and how the character feels.

[I emerald for each idea]

Pages 66–67

I Answers will vary. **Examples:**
What are mobs? Groups of living creatures or beings

[I emerald]

What types are there? Hostile, passive and neutral

[I emerald]

2 Answers will vary. Ensure the response includes information from the notes in question I.

[I emerald for each sentence up to a maximum of 3]

3 Answers will vary depending on the chosen mobs.

[I emerald for each section]

4 Answers will vary. Ensure each description contains a subheading, and that sentences are correctly constructed.

[I emerald for each mob]

Pages 68–69

I Answers will vary. [I emerald for each point up to a maximum of 3]

2 Each sentence in the paragraph should be correctly constructed and initially said aloud. The content should include ideas from question I. [I emerald for the inclusion of each idea up to a maximum of 3]

3 Answers will vary but must acknowledge these key ideas:

a) Health is how well the character is.

[I emerald]

Health is lost through physical damage.

[I emerald]

b) Hostile mobs are dangerous groups. [I emerald]
They can attack and damage the health of characters. [I emerald]

4 Answers will vary. Sentences should be correctly constructed and contain the information from the previous answer. [I emerald for each piece of information]

Pages 70–71

I Answers will vary. **Examples:**

a) They swam down to the **ancient** monument and Kim was extremely excited. [I emerald]

b) They **entered** the monument, but they knew it was very dangerous. [I emerald]

c) Suddenly, a creature **appeared**. It was a scary elder guardian. [I emerald]

2 Answers will vary. [I emerald for each suitable change up to a maximum of 4]

3 Answers will vary. [I emerald for each suitable change up to a maximum of 4]

Page 72

I Answers will vary. [I emerald for each suitable change up to a maximum of 3]

2 Answers will vary. [I emerald for each suitable change up to a maximum of 3]

TRADE IN YOUR EMERALDS!

That was quite an adventure! You did a great job helping Kim to reach the beach, where she protected Turpin and the baby turtles. After Sami's arrival, you joined our pair of heroes in the ocean for some deep-sea exploration.

Now it's your turn to prepare for an imaginary ocean adventure. Add up all the emeralds you earned throughout this book, and decide what to buy from the trader to help you on your way!

Write the total number of emeralds you earned in this box:

HMMM?

SHOP INVENTORY

- DIAMOND CHESTPLATE: 30 EMERALDS
- DIAMOND HELMET: 20 EMERALDS
- DIAMOND LEGGINGS: 25 EMERALDS
- ENCHANTED DIAMOND SWORD: 30 EMERALDS
- ENCHANTED TRIDENT: 35 EMERALDS
- SPYGLASS: 15 EMERALDS
- EYE OF ENDER: 10 EMERALDS
- HEART OF THE SEA: 15 EMERALDS
- COOKED COD: 10 EMERALDS
- COOKED SALMON: 15 EMERALDS
- CAKE: 20 EMERALDS
- ENCHANTED GOLDEN APPLE: 30 EMERALDS
- POTION OF REGENERATION: 30 EMERALDS
- POTION OF WATER BREATHING: 25 EMERALDS
- POTION OF NIGHT VISION: 25 EMERALDS

That's a lot of emeralds. Well done! Remember, just like real money, you don't need to spend it all. Sometimes it's good to save up.